D0575413

# THE INNER PLANETS

## NEIL ARDLEY

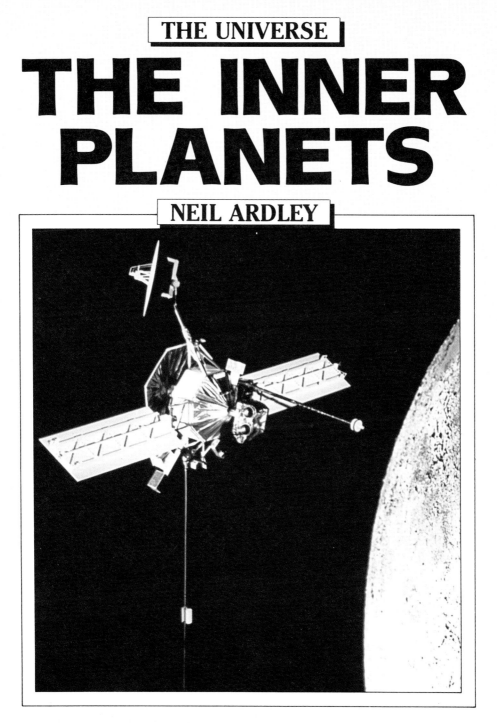

Editorial planning
**Philip Steele**

**SCHOOLHOUSE PRESS**

## Photographic credits

*t = top b = bottom l = left r = right*

**cover**: NASA

5 Science Photo Library; 6 Syndication International
Limited; 8, 9, 11, 12, 16/17, 18, 19*t* Science Photo
Library; 19*b* Frank Lane Picture Agency; 21 Science
Photo Library; 22 ZEFA; 23*t*, 23*b*, 24, 25, 28, 30, 31, 32,
33, 34, 35, 37*t* Science Photo Library; 37*b* NASA;
39, 42*t* Science Photo Library; 42*b* John Mason;
43 Science Photo Library

**Note to the reader**
In this book there are some words in the text which are printed in **bold** type. This shows that the word is listed in the glossary on page 46. The glossary gives a brief explanation of words which may be new to you.

# Contents

# Introduction

The world we live on is called the earth. It is a ball of rock, more than 7,500 miles in **diameter**. The earth is a **planet**. Planets are worlds made up of rock and **gas**. Planets move around a **star**. The path they follow through space is called an **orbit**.

Stars are made up of glowing gases which give off heat and light. Our star is called the sun. As the earth moves around the sun, it is orbited by another littler world. This is the moon. Most of the other planets have their own **moons**, too.

The sun, the planets, and the moons make up the **solar system**. The solar system appears very big to us here on the earth. It is really only a very small part of **space**. Each star in the sky is a sun, and we can see thousands of them. The whole of space and everything in it is called the **universe**.

## On the Move

Did you know that you have already traveled around the sun several times in your life? The earth takes one year to go around the sun. The earth travels at a speed of 66,875 miles per hour. As it passes through space, it spins around. Everything in space is moving.

As the planets, the moons, and the stars move through space, they pull at each other with a force called **gravity**. This force makes them stay together. If gravity stopped pulling, the planets and the moons would move away from each other. They would fly off into space.

The Solar System

Sun    Mercury  Venus    Earth    Mars              Jupiter

inner planets

## Neighbors in Space

Some of the planets which go around the sun are very near to us. Others are much farther away. We can see some of the planets in the night sky. They are lighted up by the light that comes from the sun. The planets do not give off light themselves. But they look like tiny dots of light from the earth.

This book is about the four planets that are closest to the sun. We call them the inner planets. They are Mercury, Venus, Earth, and Mars. Mercury and Venus are the ones nearest to the sun. Earth is the third planet from the sun. Mars is the fourth planet from the Sun.

▲ From earth, the planets look like stars. Here, the planet Venus is shining brightly just below the moon. As Venus travels around the sun, it comes very close to the earth. That is why we can see it so clearly.

▼ Nine planets travel around the sun. The sun gives warmth and light to the solar system. The nearest planets to the sun are very hot. The farthest planets from the sun are bitterly cold.

Saturn

Uranus

Neptune

Pluto

outer planets

# Fact and Fiction

People knew about the planets long ago. They looked up and saw that five of the stars appeared to change their position in the night sky. All the other stars appeared to stay in the same places. These moving points of light were really planets.

## Gods and Monsters

Many people who lived in ancient days thought that gods and goddesses lived in the sky. They believed that the sun and the moon were gods. They gave the moving stars the names of gods and goddesses, too.

Today, we use the names that the Romans gave to the planets. Venus was their goddess of love. Mars was their god of war. Mercury was a god who was a messanger for all the other gods. Saturn was the god of the harvest. Jupiter was the leader of the gods and goddesses. Neptune was the god of the sea and Pluto was the god of the Underworld.

▲ Mars was the Roman god of war. The planet Mars shines in the night sky with a reddish glow, the color of blood. For many years, people thought that the planet could cause wars on earth.

People thought that these planets ruled their lives. Later, people found out that the planets are other worlds. They made up new stories about the planets. Some stories said that monsters lived on them.

WHEN THE AIR-LOCK HAD BEEN RE-PRESSURISED –

N-NOW WHAT HAPPENS?

WE TALK TO IT, I SUPPOSE...

OKAY, WHATEVER YOU ARE... I'M DAN DARE. WHAT IS THE MESSAGE?

◀ For a long time, people have liked stories about space travel in the future. Stories like this are called "science fiction." In this comic strip the hero is with monsters from the planet Venus.

## Finding Out the Truth

A few people wanted to know the truth about the planets. These people were called **astronomers**. They measured how these five stars moved across the sky. The movements showed that these stars are really other worlds, lighted up by the sun.

At first, people thought that the planets and the sun all moved around the earth as the moon does. A Greek astronomer named Aristarchus did not agree. In about 260 B.C., he said that the earth and all the other planets moved around the sun. No one believed him. They thought that if the earth were moving around the sun, then we would all fall off!

In 1609, an Italian named Galileo Galilei started to use a **telescope** to watch the sky. A telescope makes distant objects look nearer. In 1728, a British astronomer named James Bradley used a telescope to prove that the earth does move around the sun. It had taken almost 2,000 years to show that Aristarchus was right after all.

Later, people using better telescopes found three more planets. Uranus was first spotted in 1781. Neptune was discovered in 1846 and Pluto in 1930. Since 1962, machines called **space probes** have been sent to almost all the planets. They have sent us close-up views of the planets. They have not seen any monsters! But they have shown us worlds which are very different from the earth.

▼ The USSR landed two Venera space probes on Venus. Machines like this help us to find out a lot about planets. Probes can find out about the surface of a planet, its air, and its clouds. The probes can tell us whether it would be safe for people to land there.

# Mercury: Next to the Sun

▼ The surface of Mercury is a rocky desert. The space probe Mariner 10 took photographs of it in 1974 and 1975. The probe also measured the temperature on Mercury and the effect of the sun's rays on the planet.

Mercury is the planet nearest to the sun. When astronomers look at Mercury through a telescope, they are looking almost straight at the sun. **Do not try to look for Mercury through a telescope yourself. The sun's rays may damage your eyes.** Mercury is hard to see in the sun's bright glare. It is small, too. This makes it hard to get a good view of Mercury from the earth. Until only a few years ago, we knew very little about Mercury.

## Talking about Planets

We try to find out as many things as possible about a planet. We study its surface to find out if it has mountains and plains. Most planets have a layer of gases above the surface. This is called the **atmosphere**. The earth's atmosphere is made of air. We can learn about the gases which surround other planets. We can measure **temperatures** on a planet to see how hot or how cold it is there.

We can figure out the size of a planet. We can measure its diameter. This is the distance through the center of the planet from one side to the other. We can also figure out its **mass**. Mass is the amount of material in a planet.

We have to know how a planet moves, too. We measure the length of the planet's year, which is the time it takes to travel around the sun. Astronomers call this the **period of revolution**. We can also figure out the length of the planet's day, which is the time it takes to spin around once. This is called the **period of rotation**. A planet spins around on its **axis**. This is an imaginary line running between the planet's most northern and southern parts, or **poles**. The axis may be tilted at an angle to the sun.

► The world's largest radio telescope is at Arecibo, on the Caribbean island of Puerto Rico. The telescope was built in a valley. This photograph was taken from the air and looks straight down at the great dish. In 1965, radio signals were sent from here to Mercury. The information which the signals bounced back from the planet showed us how the planet spins.

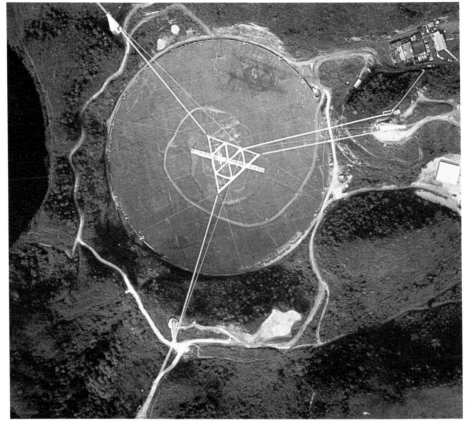

## What Is Mercury Like?

Mercury is the second smallest of the nine planets known to be orbiting the sun. Its diameter is less than half the earth's diameter. It is an airless world. There is no life there. The sun scorches the rocky surface by day. At night, the planet's temperature goes far below freezing. Mercury has no moons to shine in its sky, so it is darker at night there than it is on earth.

### Facts about Mercury

| | |
|---|---|
| **Diameter:** | 3,100 miles |
| **Mass:** | 1/16 of the earth |
| **Distance from the sun:** | 36.3 million miles |
| **Period of rotation:** | 59 days |
| **Period of revolution:** | 88 days |
| **Tilt of axis:** | 0° |
| **Gravity on the surface:** | 2/5 of the earth |
| **Average temperature:** | 662°F (day) −274°F (night) |
| **Atmosphere:** | small amount of helium |
| **Number of moons:** | none |

Earth          Mercury

# Mercury: The Space Probe

Astronomers tried to get a good look at Mercury for many years. They made some maps of the tiny planet by looking at it through big telescopes. However, the maps turned out to be wrong.

In 1973, the United States launched a space probe called Mariner 10 into space. It had no people on board. It carried two television cameras and some **instruments** to measure the planet. The probe could send pictures and signals back to the earth by **radio**.

In 1974 and 1975, Mariner 10 flew past Mercury three times. It flew as close as 205 miles to the surface. The photographs that were taken showed us a third of the planet's whole surface.

## Holes and Cracks

The photographs from Mariner 10 showed that Mercury is very much like the moon. It is mostly covered with craters, which are big, round holes in the surface. There are also ranges of mountains and large plains which have few craters. The biggest plain is called the Caloris Basin. It has a round shape and is 813 miles across.

The craters were made long ago. Large lumps of rock crashed on to Mercury from space. One huge crash made the Caloris Basin. The rocks were **asteroids**, which are like tiny planets wandering through space. Some craters were made by **comets**. Comets are balls of frozen gas and dust which travel around the sun.

Mercury also has deep cracks in its surface. One is called Discovery Scarp. It forms a giant cliff almost two miles high and 313 miles long. The cracks appeared long ago when Mercury was first formed.

It was very hot. Later, it cooled and shrank in size. This strained the surface of the planet, and the surface split open.

## An Unfriendly World

If you could land on Mercury during its long day, you would see a landscape of bare rock. The sun's light would be blinding. The heat would be like the inside of an oven. At night, it would be very cold.

Mercury has almost no atmosphere. There is just a little of the gas **helium** there, which comes from the sun. There is not enough gas in the atmosphere to block out any of the sun's rays during the day or to keep the planet warm at night.

▼ The space probe Mariner 10 passing over the rim of Mercury. The probe left the earth in 1973. It traveled past Venus and Mercury and then swung around to orbit the sun.

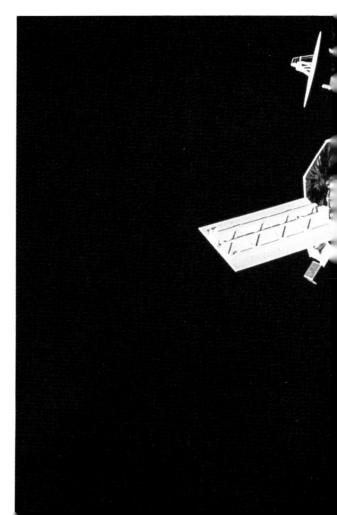

► The inside of the planet Mercury is very hot. The center, or core, contains a lot of molten iron. The core is slowly cooling and shrinking. It is about 2,375 miles in diameter. The surface of the planet is made of rock.

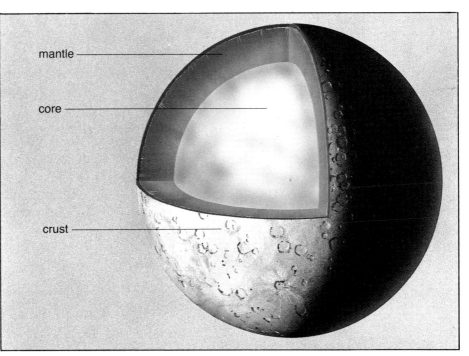

mantle

core

crust

# Venus: Our Nearest Planet

On our journey through the inner solar system, after Mercury we come next to Venus. Venus can be seen from the earth. It is often the first point of light to appear in the sky at sunset and the last to fade at sunrise. We can see Venus easily because it is very bright. Venus comes closer to the earth than any other planet. At its nearest, it is only 26 million miles away.

If you were able to look down at Venus from a spacecraft, you would see another reason that the planet is so bright. It is covered by pale clouds. In fact, you would not be able to see the surface of the planet at all.

The pale clouds kept astronomers from finding out very much about Venus for a long time. When they looked at Venus through a telescope, all they could see was that the planet has no moons. They could not tell if Venus was like the earth beneath its layer of clouds. They needed another way of finding out about the planet's secrets.

◀ Venus was photographed in 1974 by the space probe Mariner 10. The planet is covered by thick clouds. The clouds reflect the sunlight. They make the planet easy to see from the earth.

## Facts about Venus

| | |
|---|---|
| Diameter: | 7,563 miles |
| Mass: | ⅘ of the earth |
| Distance from the sun: | 67 million miles |
| Period of rotation: | 243 days |
| Period of revolution: | 225 days |
| Tilt of axis: | 2° |
| Gravity on the surface: | ⅘ of the earth |
| Average temperature: | 869°F |
| Atmosphere: | carbon dioxide |
| Number of moons: | none |

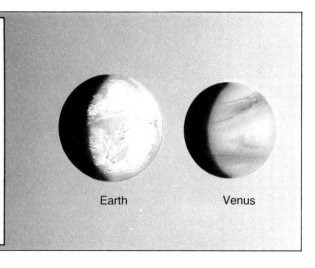

Earth          Venus

## Looking through the Clouds

Scientists use **radar** to find out about the shape and location of objects in space. Radar sends out rays. These rays are called **radio waves**. If the radio waves meet another object, they bounce back again. We can pick them up with radar equipment and find out where they are coming from.

In 1961, radar signals were sent from the earth to Venus. The signals went through the planet's clouds. They bounced off the surface of Venus and returned to the earth. They showed that Venus turns very slowly, only once in 243 days. They also showed that the planet spins backward. If we could look down over its north pole, we would see Venus spinning clockwise. All the other planets in the solar system spin the other way.

## A Changing Face

You can look at Venus through **binoculars** or a small telescope. You will probably see a crescent and not a round shape. The crescent changes shape as Venus moves around the sun. The changes are called the **phases** of Venus. We can only see the half of Venus that is lighted by the sun. When Venus is near the earth, we see only a small part of the bright half. As it gets farther away, we see more.

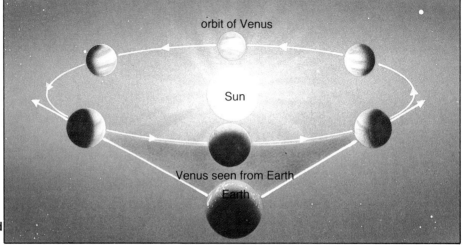

► The orbit of Venus passes close to the earth. From the earth, we see the side of Venus which is lighted up by the sun.

# Venus: An Orange Sky

The Romans named Venus after their goddess of love. Is it really a planet of love and beauty? People used to think it might be. They knew that it was close to the sun and that it was probably hot. However, they thought that the yellow clouds might shade the surface from the heat. Perhaps, there was a warm and pleasant world beneath the clouds. We now know that this could not be true.

## Clouds of Poison

The clouds of Venus float in an atmosphere, just as clouds drift in the air on the earth. You could not live in the atmosphere on Venus. It is made up of a gas called **carbon dioxide**. If this gas is not mixed with other gases, it can choke people to death.

The clouds are not made of tiny drops of water, as they are on the earth. They contain drops of **sulphuric acid**. This substance is so strong that it can eat through metal.

▲ The surface of Venus is mostly flat. It is covered with stones, boulders, and lava from volcanoes.

## The Big Crush

The carbon dioxide gas on Venus is heavy. It presses down on the surface with great force. This pressure is ninety times stronger than the pressure of the air on the earth. Even if you were able to land safely on Venus in a spacecraft, the pressure of the gas would crush you as soon as you opened the door!

## Hotter than an Oven

The clouds do not shade the surface of Venus. Instead, the gases trap the sun's heat and make the surface very hot. It is hotter on Venus than it is on Mercury, even though Mercury is closer to the sun. Venus is much hotter than an oven ever gets. Metals like lead and tin would melt on Venus.

On Venus, a desert of hot rocks lies under an orange sky. Because it is so hot, there is no water. There are **volcanoes** in certain places. They may spout out hot, liquid rock called **lava**. No life can exist in such a place.

Venus and the earth were probably similar when they first formed. Both planets had carbon dioxide and water. Why is Venus so different from our world now? It is because the heat on Venus made the water boil away. On the earth, the water was cool enough to form large oceans.

Some of the carbon dioxide was mixed into the water. Tiny plants grew in the sea. Plants took in carbon dioxide from the atmosphere and turned it into **oxygen**, which is the gas we breathe. If the earth had been nearer to the sun, it would have been like Venus.

▼ The inside of Venus is similar to that of the earth. The large core is made of iron, nickel, and other metals. The crust floats on a mantle of rock. The earth's crust is cracked, but on Venus the crust seems to be solid. The size of the two planets is almost the same.

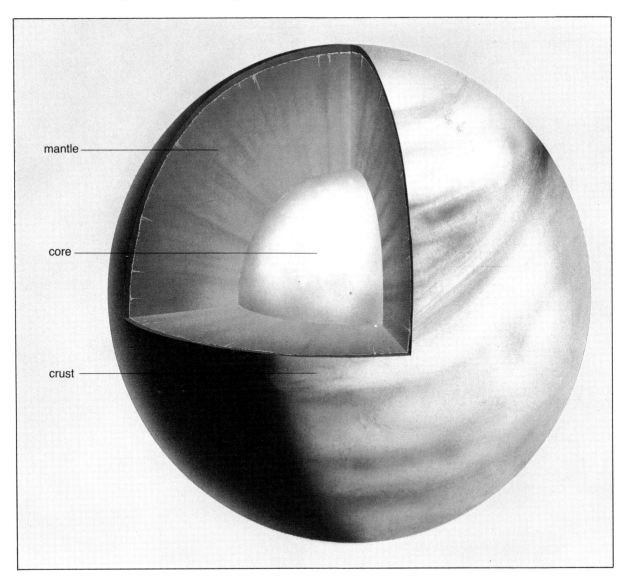

mantle

core

crust

# Venus: Probes and Maps

How do we know what Venus is like? In the 1950s, astronomers began to think that Venus might not be like the earth. They found that rays were coming from the surface of Venus. The rays could not be seen, but they could be picked up by instruments. They were a kind of ray called **microwaves**. They proved that Venus was very hot.

We had to find out more about Venus. Space probes were built to fly there. They were the first space probes to fly to any planet.

## Taking Photographs

The first two Venus probes failed. The USSR sent the first one, called Venera 1, in 1961. The probe broke down on the way. Then, the United States launched Mariner 1 to Venus. Mariner 1 blew up.

The third probe, Mariner 2, was the first to succeed. It was launched in August, 1962, and it flew past Venus in December, 1962. It measured microwaves coming from the planet's surface.

In 1974, Mariner 10 flew past Venus on its way to Mercury. It sent back photographs of the clouds. These photographs showed that very fast winds blow in the top layer of the gases which surround the planet. The winds move at 220 miles per hour.

---

▶ Pioneer Venus 1 used radar to map Venus. In this photograph, the low plains have been colored blue. Higher land has been colored green and yellow. The highest land is colored brown and red. Aphrodite Land is about the size of Africa. Ishtar Land is the size of Australia. The Maxwell Mountains are higher than Mount Everest on the earth.

Since 1967, the USSR has sent many Venera probes to Venus. Some of the early probes were crushed before they reached the surface. Then, in 1975, Venera 9 and Venera 10 landed and sent back the first photographs of the rocky surface. The probes broke down after they had been on Venus for only an hour. They may have been destroyed by the acid in the clouds.

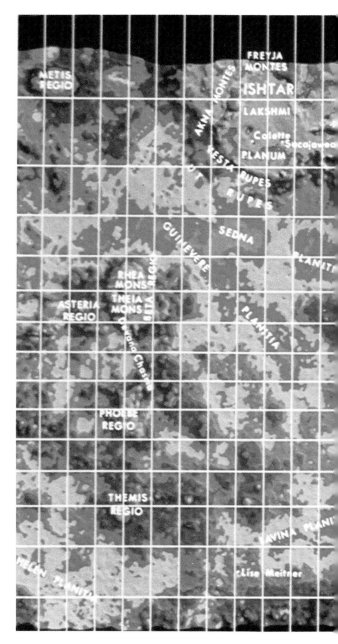

16

## Mapping Venus

In 1978, the United States sent the Pioneer Venus 1 probe to the planet. It did not land, but it went into orbit around Venus. It circled the planet for many months. Pioneer Venus 1 took photographs of the whole surface of the planet. It used radar beams to "see" through the clouds.

A map of Venus has been made from these photographs. It shows that most of Venus is a smooth plain. There are two large regions which stick up above the flat ground. They are like the land that we call **continents** on the earth. The biggest region is called Aphrodite Land. The other region is called Ishtar Land. Plans have been made to make more radar maps of Venus by using a **satellite**.

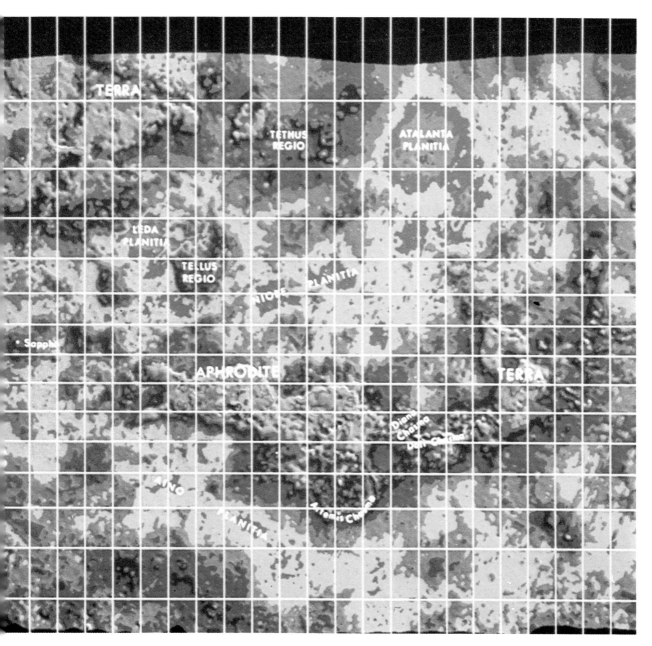

# Earth: Our Home

From space, our planet gleams like a jewel in the solar system. The sun's rays make it shine brightly. It appears bright blue, with white swirls of cloud. The blue is the color of the oceans. They take up twice as much of the earth's surface as the brown patches of land.

## Around the Sun

The movement of the earth is very important to our lives. It gives us days and nights. It is daytime in the half of the earth that faces the sun. In the other half, which is in shadow, it is night. The earth spins once in 23 hours, 56 minutes. The time between one sunrise and the next is very nearly twenty-four hours.

The time that the earth takes to go around the sun once gives us our year. It is not an exact number of days. To solve this problem, we have three years in a row each having 365 days, then the fourth year has 366 days. This year is called a **leap year**.

The earth's axis is tilted. This makes the weather change so that we have **seasons**. During the year, some parts of the earth point toward the sun. These parts get more sunshine. The days are longer and it is warm. It is summer here. The parts that are pointing away have their winter. Then, as the earth moves around its orbit, other parts start to point away from the sun. There, the season changes and winter comes.

◄ The earth as seen from space. You can see the ice and snow of Antarctica to the south. You can see the forests and deserts of Africa to the north. The blue areas are the South Atlantic Ocean and the Indian Ocean. Swirls of white cloud surround the planet.

▲ Dawn in the mountains of Italy. The sun rises above a blanket of cloud. The sun rises each day in the east and sets in the west. It brings warmth and light to our planet.

## How the Earth Was Formed

The earth was formed from a cloud of gas and dust which was floating in space. The other planets and the sun were formed from this cloud, too.

About five billion years ago, the cloud began to shrink. It also started spinning. It got faster as it got smaller. Most of the gas and dust became packed together in the middle of the cloud. Slowly, the center heated up and turned into a star, the sun.

The planets were formed about 4.6 billion years ago from the rest of the spinning cloud. In places, the dust became packed together to form balls of rock moving around the sun. Gases from the rock produced atmospheres around the planets.

▶ Autumn in North America. The northern part of the earth is now tilting away from the sun. The days are getting colder and there is less sunshine. The leaves on many trees are starting to die.

### Facts about the Earth

| | |
|---|---|
| **Diameter:** | 7,926 miles |
| **Mass:** | 5,980 billion billion tons |
| **Distance from the sun:** | 93 million miles |
| **Period of rotation:** | 23 hours, 56 minutes |
| **Period of revolution:** | 365 days, 6 hours |
| **Tilt of axis:** | 23.4° |
| **Average temperature:** | 71°F |
| **Atmosphere:** | mainly nitrogen and oxygen |
| **Number of moons** | 1 |

# Earth: Inside Our Planet

We live on the surface of the earth beneath the atmosphere. On the surface, we are on top of the earth's **crust**. This is a layer of rock around the earth, which is something like the peel of an orange. The crust beneath our feet is about eighteen miles thick. The oceans lie in huge hollows in the earth's crust. Under the oceans, the crust is only six miles thick.

Beneath the crust is another layer of rock called the **mantle**. It goes halfway down to the center of the earth. At the center, there is the earth's **core**. This is a huge ball of solid iron, about 1,550 miles in diameter. Around it is a layer of liquid iron. It is very hot inside the earth. At the center, it is about 11,000°F.

## Moving Rocks

The surface of our world is slowly changing all the time. The continents are drifting around the earth. They move about as fast as your fingernails grow.

The continents move because the earth's crust is cracked. The crust is in big pieces called **plates**. The heat from inside the earth makes the plates move. The plates carry the continents on them. In some places, the plates bump into each other, and the rocks in the crust fold up. This forms ranges of mountains such as the Rockies and the Himalayas.

At other places, the plates slide past each other or move apart. At the edges of the plates, **earthquakes** may occur when the plates slide over each other. There is a lot of pressure under the crust in many of these areas, too. In these places, there may be volcanoes. Lava may come spouting up from inside of the earth.

Rain and wind also change the earth's surface. They slowly wear down the mountains and fill the valleys with soil. This is called **erosion**.

## Earth's Magnet

The metal inside the earth makes it work like a huge **magnet**. A magnet's force comes from its two ends. The ends of the earth's magnet are near the North and South Poles. We call them the **magnetic poles**. A compass needle points to the north magnetic pole. The pull of the earth's magnet reaches out into space.

---

▶ A volcano on the island of Hawaii in the Pacific Ocean. A river of red-hot lava rolls slowly down the mountain. The lava bubbles up from thirty-one miles below the surface of the earth.

▼ Below the earth's crust are a mantle of rock and a core of iron. When the world was first formed, the heavy metals sank to the center of the spinning ball. The lighter rocks moved to the outside.

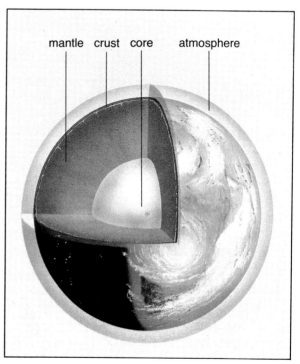

mantle  crust  core  atmosphere

# Earth: The Air around Us

The earth's atmosphere is made of air, which is a mixture of gases. Nearly four fifths of the air is a gas called **nitrogen**. Most of the rest is oxygen. There is also a small amount of a gas called **argon**, as well as a little carbon dioxide. We can breathe this mixture of gases safely.

The air contains **water vapor** also. This is water in the form of a gas. We can only see it in clouds, mist, fog, rain, hail, and snow.

The atmosphere rises about 310 miles above the earth's surface. The gases in the top part are very thin. We can only live in the bottom part where there is enough air to breathe. Even the highest places where people can live on the earth are only about four miles above sea level.

## Living Things

It is most likely that the earth is the only planet in the solar system to have life. This is because living things need oxygen and water. No other world in our solar system has oxygen.

Even carbon dioxide, which can poison people if there is too much of it, plays its part in keeping things alive on the earth. In daylight, plants take in carbon dioxide and water. The plants change these into oxygen and food for themselves. This is how plants grow. Animals and people can use the plants as food. They can breathe in the oxygen which the plants give off.

Often, people **pollute** the air around them. Fumes from cars and factories enter the air. The fumes may contain poisons which can kill plants and animals.

▼ The surface of the earth is covered with plant life and teeming with animals. Life on the earth needs oxygen, water, and sunlight. If we pollute the air, water, and soil, we may destroy many forms of life.

The atmosphere keeps us alive in many ways. It keeps harmful rays given off by the sun from reaching the ground. The air lets through the light and heat rays that we need to live.

## Wind and Waves

The sun's heat warms the ground. The air next to the ground gets warm. The warm air rises. Cold air moves in to take its place. The moving air is wind. The sun's heat also warms the oceans and makes water flow from warm places to cold places. These movements are called ocean **currents**.

▶ Here, the Space Shuttle is being fitted with special tiles, so it will not burn up in the atmosphere. The layer of gases around the earth acts as a barrier. If a small rock from space enters the atmosphere, it slows down and is soon burned up. A spacecraft which returns to the earth must also pass through the atmosphere.

▶ Tiny particles from the sun stream through space. When they reach the earth, they are trapped by the magnetic pull of the planet. The particles strike the gases in the earth's atmosphere. This causes patterns of color to form around the earth's poles, which we call the Northern or Southern Lights.

# Earth: Out into Space

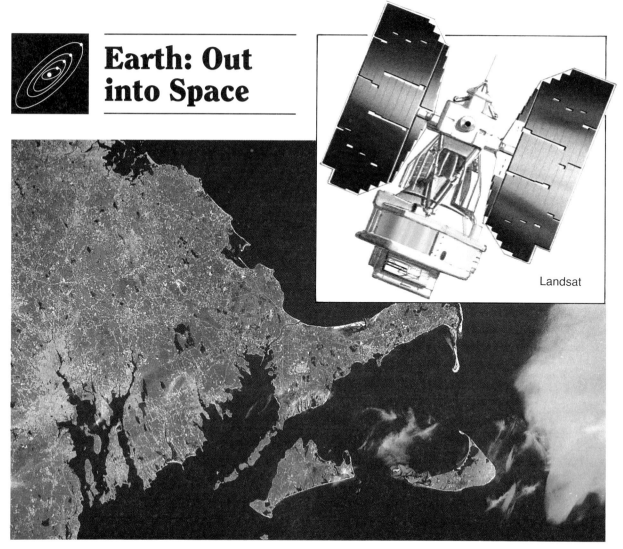

Landsat

A satellite is any small object which travels around a bigger one in space. The moon is a satellite of the earth. Machines that we orbit around our planet are satellites also.

The satellites we make are often launched into space by **rockets**. A rocket moves very fast. It reaches a speed of 17,625 miles per hour. Then, a rocket lets go of a satellite, which moves into orbit around the earth. Sometimes, satellites are put into orbit by a **Space Shuttle**. This spacecraft is launched by a rocket. When the Space Shuttle is in space, it lets go of the satellite. Later, the Shuttle returns to the earth like an airplane.

▲ This computer photograph of Cape Cod, Massachusetts, was taken by a Landsat satellite (inset). Landsat pictures can be given colors to show towns, plant life, pollution, or other points of interest. The United States launched five Landsats between 1972 and 1984.

▶ Very strong beams of light can be sent through space by machines called lasars. Here, a laser beam is being beamed from the earth to a satellite in space. The satellite reflects the beam back to lasers on the earth. Scientists can time the beam from different parts of the earth in order to measure movements in the earth's crust. This picture was taken over a long period of time. The stars appear as streaks of light.

## Around the Earth

Satellites keep moving because there is no air in space to make them slow down and stop. Satellites, like the moon, are held in orbit by the pull of the earth's gravity. Many satellites orbit 22,438 miles above the earth. Because the earth spins, or rotates, the satellites stay in the same place in orbit. This makes it easy to send radio signals between the satellite and the ground.

## At Work in Space

The first satellite was launched from the earth in 1957. It was made by the USSR and called Sputnik 1. The second satellite, Sputnik 2, contained a dog named Laika. She was sent up to find out if living things could travel safely in space.

Since then, thousands of satellites have been launched by many different countries. A few of them have carried people. These machines make use of space in many ways.

Many satellites are used to look down on our planet. Some send back photographs of the clouds below. These photographs help us to make weather forecasts. Other satellites send back photographs of the earth's surface. These can tell us where large groups of fish can be found in the ocean. They can help us to find oil, coal, or metals which we can mine. They can warn us if crops are not growing well in any part of the world.

Other satellites look outward into space. They can measure distant stars and send back signals to the earth.

Some satellites use radio signals to carry telephone calls or television programs. Radio signals can be bounced from one side of the earth to the other. Satellites can link up people all over the world. Some satellites send signals that can tell people where they are on the earth. The signals can be used by people on ships or in aircraft to check their positions.

# The Moon: Our Partner

The moon is the earth's partner in space. Both worlds go around the sun together as the moon whirls around the earth. Some of the other planets have moons orbiting them, too.

When we look at the moon from the earth, we always see the same side. There is another side that never faces the earth. This is because the moon spins around once in just the same period of time that it takes to go around the earth.

## The Moon's Face

The moon appears to change shape as the days go by. Sometimes, it has a thin, curved shape, or crescent. We call this a **new moon** or an old moon, depending on the point in the moon's revolution. Sometimes, it looks like a whole circle. We call this a **full moon**. In between, it looks like a half-circle. The changes happen as the moon moves around the earth. We see other parts of the moon lighted by the sun.

The changes in the moon's shape are called the **phases** of the moon. It takes twenty-nine days for the moon to go through all its phases from new moon to full moon and back to new moon.

## Shadows in Space

Sometimes, an eclipse of the moon takes place. The moon passes through the earth's shadow. The moon can hardly be seen for about an hour. There are usually two or three eclipses of the moon each year.

You may see an eclipse of the sun also. This happens when the moon's shadow touches the earth's surface. The moon may blot out the sun for a few minutes.

## Pulling Power

The earth and moon are partners in space because their gravity holds them together. The moon's gravity causes the **tides** in the earth's oceans. The moon pulls at the earth. This makes the water rise higher, as tides. The sun's gravity also helps make the tides on the earth.

The tides rise and fall twice a day as the earth spins. A high tide happens on each side of the earth when the moon passes overhead. As the water is pulled up in one place, it falls in another place. This is a low tide.

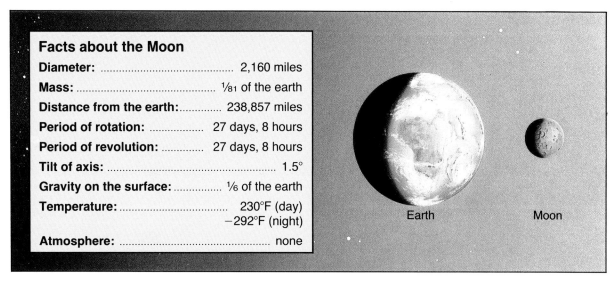

**Facts about the Moon**

| | |
|---|---|
| **Diameter:** | 2,160 miles |
| **Mass:** | 1/81 of the earth |
| **Distance from the earth:** | 238,857 miles |
| **Period of rotation:** | 27 days, 8 hours |
| **Period of revolution:** | 27 days, 8 hours |
| **Tilt of axis:** | 1.5° |
| **Gravity on the surface:** | 1/6 of the earth |
| **Temperature:** | 230°F (day) −292°F (night) |
| **Atmosphere:** | none |

Earth          Moon

▼ The moon reflects light from the sun. From the earth, we see different amounts of light and shadow on the moon. This makes the moon seem to change shape during the course of a month.

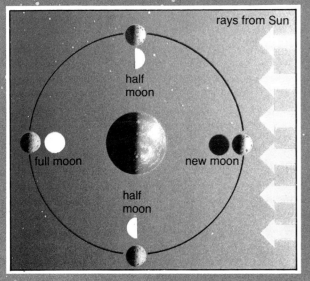

rays from Sun

half moon

full moon

new moon

half moon

Earth's shadow

Moon's orbit

Earth

Moon

Sun

In an eclipse of the moon, the earth blocks off the sun's rays. The moon disappears in the shadow.

# The Moon: Bare Rock

No one knows for certain how the moon was formed. Perhaps, it split away from the earth. Perhaps, it was formed in space on its own.

It is more likely that the moon was formed when another planet about the size of Mars crashed into the earth. This may have happened soon after all the planets were formed. At this time, both the earth and the other planets would have been made of hot liquid rock. The crash would have made some of this rock splash out into space. The drops came together and hardened to form the moon.

The moon, like the earth, has a crust, mantle, and a core. The moon's crust does not move. The moon is a world that does not change.

## The Surface

There is an old saying that the moon is made of green cheese. In fact, there is only bare rock on the moon. The surface is covered with dark dust. It is true, however, that the surface is full of holes like Swiss cheese! The holes are craters of all sizes. There are big craters with high walls. These form the moon's mountains.

There are also large plains. Long ago, astronomers thought that they looked like water. They gave the plains the names of seas and oceans. Today, we know that the plains are not covered by water.

When the moon was young, many large rocks crashed into it from space. Each crash caused a crater to form. Very big rocks cracked the surface. Lava flowed out and hardened to form the plains. The moon has looked the same ever since then.

▼ The earth rises above the rim of the moon. The earth reflects light from the sun. Sunlight also lights up the rocky surface of the moon. The moon is empty and still.

► This map shows the side of the moon we can see from the earth. It shows plains, mountains, and some of the moon's hundreds of thousands of craters. The largest crater is called Clavius. It is 144 miles wide.

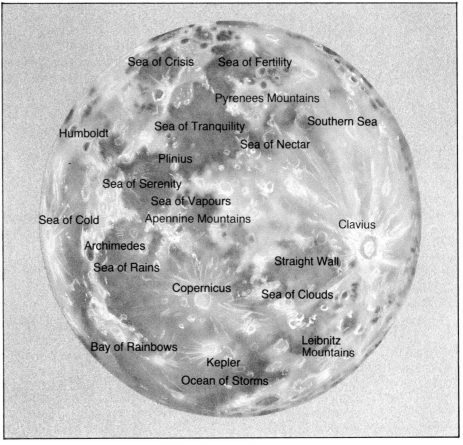

Sea of Crisis  Sea of Fertility

Pyrenees Mountains

Southern Sea

Humboldt    Sea of Tranquility

Sea of Nectar

Plinius

Sea of Serenity

Sea of Vapours

Sea of Cold    Apennine Mountains

Clavius

Archimedes

Straight Wall

Sea of Rains

Copernicus    Sea of Clouds

Leibnitz
Mountains

Bay of Rainbows

Kepler

Ocean of Storms

## Walking on the Moon

If you could land on the moon, you could walk around easily. The moon's gravity is six times less than the gravity on the earth. This is because the moon is smaller than the earth, so it has less pulling power. On the moon, your body would weigh six times less than on the earth.

The moon has no atmosphere. If you went to the moon, you would have to wear a **spacesuit**. This would carry air for you to breathe, and it would protect you from the heat of the sun. You would have a radio in your spacesuit, so you could talk to other people. There is no air to carry sound.

A moon day lasts for two earth weeks. The sun shines down on the moon all the time during its day. The moon's surface gets hotter than boiling water. During its night, it gets much colder than freezing.

▼ The metals and rocks inside the moon form a crust and a mantle around the central core.

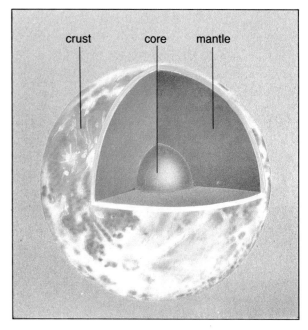

crust    core    mantle

# The Moon: Touchdown

For hundreds of years, people dreamed of going to the moon. Stories were told of people who traveled to the moon in all kinds of ways. Some were blown there by a whirlwind. Others flew there on the backs of geese, or were shot from a huge cannon. The stories told how the travelers found strange creatures living there.

All these ideas vanished in 1966. A Russian space probe called Luna 9 landed on the moon. It sent back the first photograph of the surface. This showed an empty land, which was covered with rocks. Nothing lived there.

## Getting Ready

Space probes went to the moon before people flew there. Some probes took photographs of the surface from space. Other probes landed to check that people could go and walk safely on the moon.

While these probes were doing their work, people were testing spacecraft. First, they tried them out in the space around the earth. Then, they flew them around the moon. People who travel in space are called **astronauts**.

## Moon Landings

On July 20, 1969, two American astronauts landed on the moon. It had taken them three days to fly to the moon. They landed on the moon in a **lunar module**. This was a part of a bigger spacecraft which stayed in orbit around the moon.

▶ The Apollo 11 flights to the moon began with the launch of this giant rocket called Saturn V. It lifted the spacecraft out of the earth's atmosphere.

The astronauts were on the moon for twenty-one and a half hours. During this time, they walked around on the surface for two and a half hours. Then, they left in the lunar module. They joined up with the main spacecraft and returned to the earth.

The first moon landing flight was called Apollo 11. Later, there were five more Apollo flights to the moon. They all made landings. During three of the later landings, the astronauts used a special moon car to drive around on the surface. They collected soil and pieces of rock.

▼ Tire marks and footprints on the surface of the moon. Cars called Lunar Rovers were used during the Apollo 15, 16, and 17 landings on the moon. They were powered by batteries.

The USSR used space probes to explore the moon. They sent three Luna probes to land on the moon. The probes brought soil back to the earth. Scientists have studied the soil and rock to find out what the moon is made of. In a short time, we have found out all kinds of facts about the moon.

In the future, people may return to the moon. They might build a base there, where people could live and work.

▼ Back on the earth, rock collected from the moon is weighed and measured. Over 835 pounds of rock were brought back from the moon by American astronauts.

# Mars: The Red Planet

On our journey through the inner solar system, the next planet we come to is Mars. This is the fourth planet from the sun. When Mars is near the earth, it shines like a bright red star in the sky. If you look at Mars through a big telescope, you see an orange-red disk. It has light and dark markings, and there are two white caps at the poles.

## The Big Freeze

The days and nights on Mars last almost the same period of time as they do on the earth. The tilt of the axis is almost the same, too, so Mars has real seasons. Mars takes longer to go around the sun, so the summer and the winter last nearly twice as long as they do on the earth. It is very cold on Mars because it is farther from the sun than the earth is. The temperature seldom gets above freezing there, even on a summer day.

At the north pole, there is an ice cap throughout the year. There is a white cap at the south pole, too. This cap is made up

of carbon dioxide, which is the gas in the atmosphere on Mars. It is so cold at the south pole that the gas freezes. It becomes solid and white like snow.

During the cold autumn and the colder winter, the white caps grow very large. The gas starts to fall like snow. This "snow" turns back into gas when it gets warmer. In the spring and the summer, each cap gets smaller.

| Facts about Mars | |
|---|---|
| Diameter: | 4,200 miles |
| Mass: | 1/10 of the earth |
| Distance from the sun: | 143 million miles |
| Period of rotation: | 24 hours, 37 minutes |
| Period of revolution: | 687 days |
| Tilt of axis: | 24° |
| Gravity on the surface: | 2/5 of the earth |
| Average temperature: | −9.5°F |
| Atmosphere: | carbon dioxide |
| Number of moons: | 2 |

Earth          Mars

◄ Mars is the third brightest planet in our sky. Its orbit brings it to within 34 million miles of our planet. From the earth, it looks like a bright star.

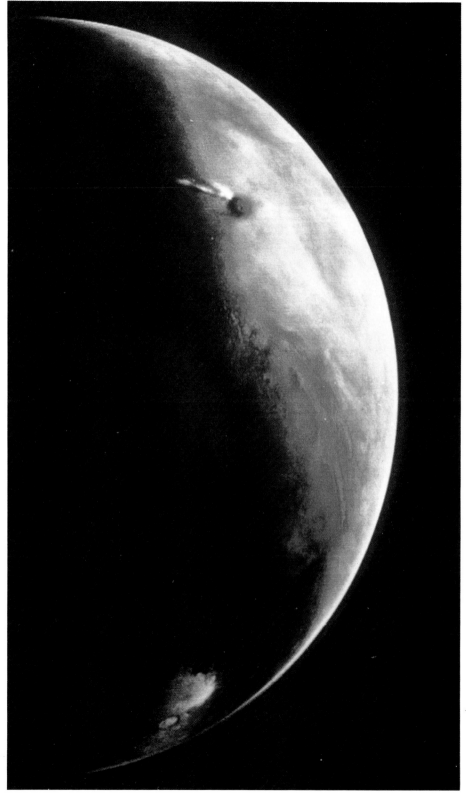

► The planet Mars reflects light from the sun, which is 142 million miles away. On the right, we can see the frozen carbon dioxide around the planet's south pole and a volcano to the north.

# Mars: Canyons and Volcanoes

Mars was formed about 4.6 billion years ago at the same time as the other planets in our solar system. Dust floating in space gathered together. The dust became a ball of rock. At first, the rock was so hot that it was liquid. Then, it cooled and hardened.

Today, astronomers think that Mars has a thick crust and a small core. The crust is made up of rocks that contain iron. The rocks are red, which is why Mars looks red.

When Mars was young, volcanoes burst through the planet's surface. They spouted gases that formed the atmosphere. Water vapor was in these gases. The surface of Mars was so cold that the water vapor could not turn into liquid water. Because of this, Mars never had any oceans.

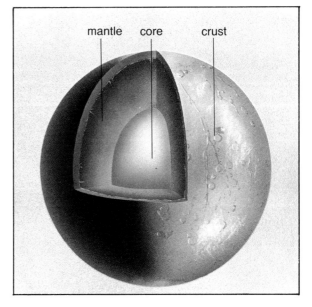

mantle　core　crust

▲ The rocks inside the planet Mars form an outer crust, a mantle, and an inner core. The red color of the planet shows that the crust contains a great deal of iron.

▼ A space probe called Viking 1 Lander took this photograph of Mars. It showed a surface covered with red rocks.

# A Strange World

If you could fly around Mars, you would see many unusual sights. There are valleys far deeper than the Grand Canyon. The valleys have been formed by movements in the planet's crust. They never carried water like the canyons on the earth. There are mountains much higher than Mount Everest, which is the highest mountain on earth. The mountains on Mars are made of huge piles of lava. They are old volcanoes. There are also large craters in many places. These were made when big rocks crashed into Mars long ago.

The orange-red surface of Mars is covered by rocks. Among the rocks are **dunes**. These are banks of red sand that blows around in the strong wind. Sometimes, there are vast dust storms. They hide the surface of the planet from view.

The dust storms can make markings appear on the planet. Once, astronomers thought that they could see long thin lines on the surface of Mars. They thought that these lines were canals. They wondered if the canals could have been built by people to carry water from the poles. Today, we know there are no canals on Mars. There are just shifting patterns of sand.

# A Pink Sky

Perhaps, the most unusual sight on Mars is its pink sky. It is pink because red dust floats in the atmosphere. Most of the atmosphere is made up of carbon dioxide. There are also small amounts of nitrogen, argon, and some water vapor. There is hardly any oxygen at all. The gases around Mars do not shield the planet from the sun's rays. Many of these rays are harmful. It would be hard for life to exist on such a planet.

▼ The Viking probes photographed huge volcanoes on Mars. They are no longer pouring out lava, but they might erupt again some day.

# Mars: In Search of Life

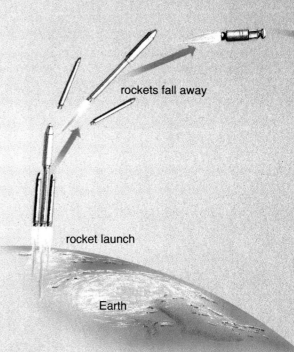

▼ The Viking probes were launched in 1975. They were lifted into space by rockets. It took them ten months to reach Mars. A lander section flew down to the planet's surface. The rest of the probe went into orbit around Mars.

rockets fall away

rocket launch

Earth

When people on the earth saw the icy caps on Mars through their telescopes, they thought that there must be water there. Living things need water. So people wondered if there might be Martians living in cities on the red planet.

## Space Probes

There was only one way to find out whether or not life existed on Mars. That was to send space probes to explore the planet.

The United States has sent the most probes to Mars. The first one was called Mariner 4. It passed by Mars in 1965. It was followed by Mariners 6 and 7 in 1969. These probes sent back photographs which showed craters on the surface. It appeared that Mars must be just like the moon.

Then, in 1971, Mariner 9 went into orbit around Mars. It sent back photographs of the whole surface. These showed the big canyons and volcanoes on Mars. In 1976, two Viking probes landed on Mars. They sent back more photographs of the surface. They searched for signs of life.

## Looking for Clues

The Viking probes were well equipped to detect life. When they arrived at the planet, some of the probes split into two sections. One section of the probes went into orbit around Mars. From there, the cameras could have spotted any Martian cities. The probes could have found any sources of heat or water being used by Martians. They found no sign of life.

The two sections of the probes which landed would have spotted any Martians on the surface. Again, none were seen. This was not a surprise because people now knew that Mars was a very harsh world. Still, there might have been tiny **microbes** living in the soil. The Viking landers scraped up some soil and tested it for microbes. No microbes were found.

This does not prove that Mars is without life. There may be life somewhere else on Mars. Or it could be that there has been life on Mars in the past. There are channels on the surface of Mars that look like dry river beds. Liquid water flowed there long ago, when heat from volcanoes melted the ice in the ground. Perhaps living things once used this water.

The United States and the USSR will send more space probes to Mars in the next few years. In the next century, people may be able to fly to Mars and land there.

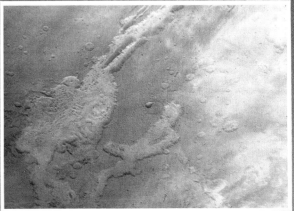

▲ Mariner and Viking probes have taken photographs of the Valles Marineris. These are deep canyons which stretch for thousands of miles across the surface of Mars.

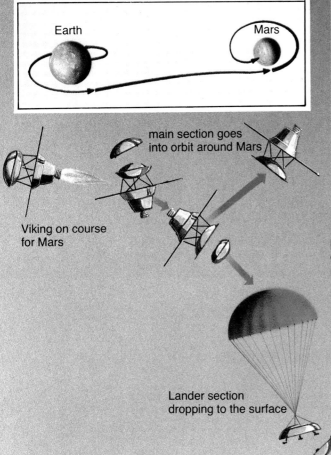

Earth

Mars

Viking on course for Mars

main section goes into orbit around Mars

Lander section dropping to the surface

Mars

▼ The Viking landers carried television cameras and an arm for collecting soil from the surface. They measured the temperature and the speed of the winds and carried out other tests.

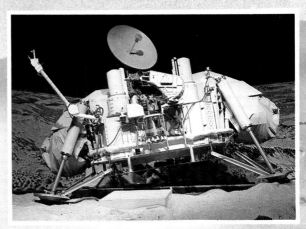

# The Moons of Mars

Mars has two moons. An American astronomer named Asaph Hall discovered them in 1877. The moons are called Phobos and Deimos. They are the Greek names for the sons of the god of war. The names mean "fear" and "panic."

## Tiny Worlds

Phobos and Deimos are both tiny worlds. They are very much smaller than our moon. They look like flying potatoes, and each one is about the size of a city on the earth. Phobos is sixteen miles long and twelve miles wide. Deimos is nine miles long and eight miles wide.

Phobos orbits at a distance from Mars of 5,860 miles. One orbit takes only 7 hours, 39 minutes. Deimos is at a distance of 14,690 miles from Mars. It takes 30 hours, 18 minutes to go around its planet. Astronomers think that Phobos might break up into pieces some day. The pieces would stay in orbit and form a ring around Mars.

▼ As Mars travels around the sun, it is circled by Phobos and Deimos. These tiny moons orbit Mars counterclockwise. Phobos is slowly losing height.

Mars

Phobos

Deimos

orbit of Mars

▶ Phobos has a lumpy shape. Other rocks have crashed into this tiny moon and left deep craters and scars on the surface.

## What Are the Moons?

Phobos and Deimos are dark lumps of rock. They are dotted with craters. Phobos also has deep channels. These may be cracks in the surface. Deimos has a very weak force of gravity. Both tiny satellites may once have been asteroids and not moons at all. If this is the case, then they may have come near Mars. The planet's gravity then pulled at them, and they could not escape. Now, they travel around Mars.

## Moon Probes

In 1988, two space probes built by the USSR and eight European nations will fly to Phobos. The probes will hover over the surface. Sections of the probes will land on the moons.

The probes may tell us how the solar system was formed. They will study the rock from which Phobos and Deimos are made. The rock may not have changed since the solar system first formed.

# Mini-planets

If we travel beyond Mars, we would come to the first of the outer planets, which is Jupiter. In between Mars and Jupiter we would find many of the tiny planets known as asteroids. This part of space is called the **asteroid belt**. The people who first discovered the asteroids named many of them after Roman and Greek gods and goddesses.

The asteroids are like big lumps of rock or metal moving through space. The biggest one, Ceres, is over 672 miles in diameter. Most of the asteroids are just a few miles in diameter.

Asteroids move around the sun, just as the bigger planets do. Most of them stay in orbit between Mars and Jupiter in the asteroid belt. Some do stray from this part of space, however.

Eros has an orbit which takes it between Mars and the earth. Hermes can come almost as close to the earth as the moon. Hidalgo travels out as far as Saturn. Icarus comes closer to the sun than Mercury. When it does, some people think it might become red hot.

▼ The mini-planets are in orbit around the sun. They are very small compared to the size of our moon. Astronomers keep track of about 3,000 asteroids, but there are countless others which are too small to record.

Ceres   Pallas   Vesta   Juno   Eros   Hidalgo   Icarus   Hermes

size of Earth's Moon

## Facts about Asteroids

| Name | Diameter | Date discovered |
| --- | --- | --- |
| Ceres | 627 miles | 1801 |
| Pallas | 380 miles | 1802 |
| Juno | 154 miles | 1804 |
| Vesta | 336 miles | 1807 |
| Eros | 14 miles | 1898 |
| Hidalgo | 9 miles | 1920 |
| Hermes | 0.3 miles | 1937 |
| Icarus | 0.6 miles | 1949 |

## Secrets to Find Out

We can spot asteroids by taking photographs of the night sky. The movement of an asteroid shows up as a trail on the photograph. No space probes have yet visited an asteroid, so we do not have any good views of them. We think that asteroids will probably look like the moons of Mars.

The asteroids were formed from the same cloud of dust that gave birth to the planets. Clumps of dust gathered together to form rocks. It may have been that the strong pull of Jupiter's gravity kept them from forming into larger worlds. Jupiter's gravity may have sent the rocks moving along different paths through space. Often, they may have crashed into one another.

Asteroids have very dark surfaces. They may contain dust that has been there since the solar system was formed. If we explore the asteroids, we may find clues about how the earth began.

▼ The asteroid belt lies between Mars and Jupiter. It divides the inner planets from the outer planets. Some asteroids have orbits which take them outside the asteroid belt. They make long journeys through the solar system.

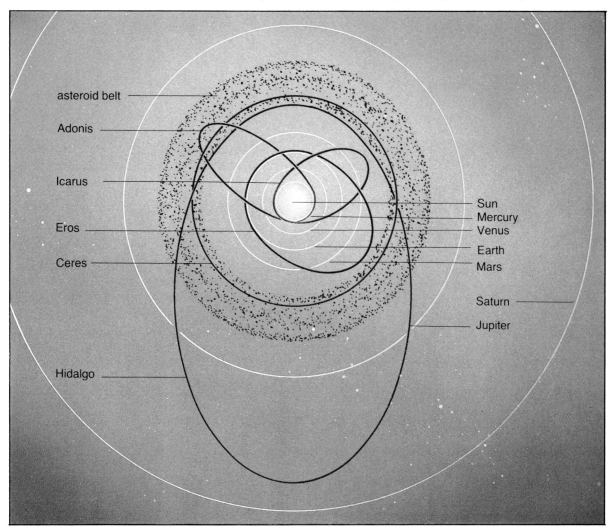

asteroid belt

Adonis

Icarus

Eros

Ceres

Hidalgo

Sun
Mercury
Venus
Earth
Mars
Saturn
Jupiter

# Space Rocks

▼ Meteor showers occur when the earth's orbit passes through a cloud of meteoroids. As the meteors burn up, we see them on earth as shooting stars.

Some asteroids come near our planet. They do not usually crash into it, because space is very large, and asteroids are very small.

Thousands of tiny bits of rock or metal do strike the earth every day. These pieces are called **meteorites**. Most of them burn up as they enter the upper layers of gas around the earth. We may see one as a bright streak of light which races through the sky for a second or two. As it burns up, it is called a **meteor**. Some people call them shooting stars or falling stars.

You should see shooting stars any night if you look for them long enough. Many can be seen during periods of meteor showers. The best showers occur around the eleventh of August and the twenty-second of December each year.

**Meteoroids**, the name for meteors in space, are made when asteroids crash into each other and break up into pieces. Meteoroids may also come from comets.

▼ Meteorites have been found in many parts of the world. The largest one on record is at Hoba West, near Grootfontein in southern Africa. It is thought to weigh about sixty-five tons.

# Earth Craters

Some meteoroids are very big. They do not burn up as they fall through the air of the earth. They fall to the surface of the earth as meteorites. Most fall into the oceans and other places where people do not live. A few meteorites are seen each year.

Meteorites are made of stone or iron. They were made when the solar system was formed. Most of them crashed into the earth, the moon, and the other planets. They made the many craters we can see on the moon, on Mercury, and on Mars.

On the earth, most of the craters have gone. The weather has worn them away. There are a few craters that still exist. The best-known ones are Meteor Crater in Arizona and Wolf Creek Crater in Australia. In 1908, there was a huge explosion in a forest deep in Siberia in the USSR. It destroyed many trees for miles around. It is probable that the explosion was caused by a meteorite from a comet hitting the earth's surface.

---

▼ About 20,000 years ago, a very large meteorite crashed into the earth. It left a hole about a half mile wide in the desert where it landed. The crater can still be seen today near the town of Canyon Diablo in Arizona. It is called Meteor Crater.

# New Worlds

What is our future in space? Will people spread out through the inner solar system? The USSR already has a **space station** called MIR. Space stations are spacecraft which orbit the earth. People can live and work in them. The United States plans to build a space station in the 1990s. People could start out from the space stations to explore other worlds.

It is probable that people will go back to the moon some day. Astronauts might fly to Mars, also. Bases could be built on these worlds for people to live in. There are plans for all this to happen in the next forty years.

In the future, spacecraft might fly to the asteroids. The spacecraft could set up machines to mine metals from these rocks. Scientists and engineers might even try to change the atmosphere of Mars and Venus. They might try to make them more like the earth, so that people could live there.

How will people make use of space in the distant future? Here, machines are being used to mine rocks from asteroids. Other machines carry the rocks back to a huge spacecraft. Perhaps, this will never happen, but many past dreams about space have already become true.

# Glossary

**argon:** a gas found around some planets. It has no color and no smell.

**asteroid:** a tiny planet made of lumpy rock which orbits the sun.

**asteroid belt:** a part of space between Mars and Jupiter where there are thousands of asteroids.

**astronaut:** a person who travels in space. Russian astronauts are known as cosmonauts.

**astronomer:** someone who studies the stars, the planets, and other objects in space.

**atmosphere:** the layer of gases which surrounds a planet or star. The earth's atmosphere is the air.

**axis:** an imaginary straight line from the top to the bottom of a spinning object, such as the earth. The object turns or rotates around this line.

**binoculars:** a kind of double telescope with two eyepieces.

**carbon dioxide:** a gas without color or smell. It is found in the air on the earth and in the atmospheres of some other planets.

**comet:** a ball of dust and ice which travels around the sun. Some of the dust streams out behind the comet to make a tail.

**continent:** a large mass of dry land on the planet earth.

**core:** the center of something.

**crescent:** a thin, curved shape. It is like the bright section of a moon when only a part of it is lighted up by the sun.

**crust:** the outer layer of rock around a planet or moon.

**current:** a movement of water or air.

**diameter:** the width of a circle or sphere. This is measured from one point on the outside, through the center, to a point on the opposite side.

**dune:** a high bank of sand, which is built up by the wind.

**dust:** tiny pieces of solid matter. A lot of dust floats around in space.

**earthquake:** a sudden shaking of the land due to movements in the top layer of rock around the earth.

**eclipse:** the shadow caused by one object blocking off the light of another. In an eclipse of the sun, the moon comes between the sun and the earth. In an eclipse of the moon, the shadow of the earth falls across the moon.

**erosion:** the wearing away of land by water, ice, and wind. The sea wears away rocks and cliffs. The wind erodes the land by blowing away sand and soil.

**full moon:** describes the moon when the whole of the surface we see is lit up by the sun. It looks like a full circle.

**gas:** a light substance that is neither liquid nor solid. Air is made up of several gases.

**gravity:** the force that pulls objects toward each other. The sun's gravity keeps the earth in orbit around it. The earth's gravity keeps us on the earth. Gravity makes objects fall and gives them weight.

**helium:** the second lightest gas of all. It is found in the sun and many parts of the universe.

**instrument:** a tool or machine made by people to help them do something. A telescope is an instrument which helps us see a long way.

**lava:** hot, liquid rock that flows up from deep inside a planet. The lava cools and hardens when it comes to the surface.

**leap year:** an earth year of 366 days. Most years have 365 days, but every fourth year has an extra day in February. This is because the earth really takes 365 days, 6 hours to go around the sun.

**lunar module:** part of a spacecraft used for exploring the moon.

**magnet:** a piece of metal that attracts objects made of iron or steel toward it.

**magnetic pole:** one of the points on the earth near the North and South Poles which direct the needle of a compass. The magnetic poles move slightly over periods of time.

**mantle:** the layer of rock between the outer shell of a planet and its central part.

**mass:** the amount of matter in an object. Mass is not affected by gravity. It does not change if the object is on the earth or in space. It is different from weight, which is affected by gravity.

**meteor:** describes a piece of rock from space when it burns up as it strikes the layer of gases around a planet. As it burns, it makes a bright light in the sky. A shooting star.

**meteorite:** describes a piece of rock or metal from space when it passes through a planet's atmosphere without burning up, and crashes on the surface of the planet.

**meteoroid:** describes a piece of rock or metal as it travels through space. Some are very large. Others are the size of pebbles.

**microbe:** a tiny living organism that can only be seen with a microscope.

**microwave:** a kind of radio wave.

**moon:** a smaller body that travels around a planet. The planet Jupiter has sixteen moons. The earth has only one moon. Most planets have moons.

**new moon:** the moon when only the edge that we see is lighted up by the sun. It looks like a thin curve. Also refers to the moon when it cannot be seen at all.

**nitrogen:** a gas found in the atmosphere of some planets. It has no color, smell, or taste. It does not burn.

**orbit:** a path through space followed by one thing going around another. The earth moves in orbit around the sun.

**oxygen:** a gas found in air and water. Oxygen is very important to all plants and animals. We cannot breathe without oxygen.

**period of revolution:** the time it takes for a planet or other object to travel once around another object.

**period of rotation:** the time it takes for a planet or other object to spin around once.

**phases:** the changes in the apparent shape of a moon or planet made by the reflection of the sun's light.

**planet:** a large body in space which moves around a star like the sun. The planet shines by reflecting the light of the star.

**plate:** a section of the earth's outer section.

**poles:** the most northern or southern points on a star, planet, or moon. They are the end points of the axis.

**pollute:** to spoil the earth and its atmosphere with waste and poison.

**radar:** a way of finding out the position and distance of an object. Radar is short for radio detection and ranging. Radio waves are sent out. When they meet an object, they bounce back to the radar set.

**radio:** a way of sending signals through air or space. It uses radio waves.

**radio wave:** a type of wave which is given off by many objects in space. Radio waves have the longest wavelengths of all rays, from a fraction of an inch to many miles.

**rocket:** something made to move forward or upward very quickly. Rockets are shaped like cylinders and are used for launching spacecraft.

**satellite:** a small body in orbit around a larger body in space. The moon is a satellite of the earth. We also call machines that orbit the earth satellites.

**seasons:** one of the four periods during the year which has a certain type of weather.

**solar system:** the sun, and all the objects that orbit it, such as the planets and their moons.

**space:** the area between the planets and the stars. Space is almost empty. It contains only tiny amounts of gas and dust.

**space probe:** a machine sent from the earth to study objects in space. It does not have people on board.

**Space Shuttle:** a spacecraft made by the United States. It can glide back to the earth and land like an airplane.

**space station:** a spacecraft which is permanently in orbit around the earth. It is big enough for people to live and work on board.

**spacesuit:** clothing designed to keep people alive in space. It gives them air to breathe and protects them from heat and small meteoroids.

**sulphuric acid:** a liquid chemical that can destroy living things and eat through metals.

**telescope:** an instrument for looking at distant objects, or for picking up some of the rays that come from them.

**temperature:** a measure of how hot or cold something is.

**tide:** a rising and falling in the level of the oceans on the earth caused by the pull of the moon's gravity and the sun's gravity.

**universe:** all of space and everything in it.

**volcano:** a type of mountain. Volcanoes are formed when very hot, liquid rock is forced up from deep inside a planet. The liquid cools and leaves a mountain of rock.

**water vapor:** water in the form of a gas.

# Index